D0454479

SEA
CREATURES

Text: Helen Cooney
Illustrations: Simone End
Consultants: Professor Frank H. Talbot and Dr. James G. Mead

Published by
The National Geographic Society
Gilbert M. Grosvenor, President and Chairman of the Board
Nina D. Hoffman, Senior Vice President
William R. Gray, Vice President and Director, Book Division
Barbara Lalicki, Director of Children's Publishing
Barbara Brownell, Senior Editor
Mark A. Caraluzzi, Marketing Manager
Vincent P. Ryan, Manufacturing Manager

Library of Congress Catalog Number: 96-068036

ISBN: 0-7922-3421-9

[Produced for the National Geographic Society by Weldon Owen Pty Ltd
43 Victoria Street, McMahons Point, NSW 2060, Australia
A member of the Weldon Owen Group of Companies
Sydney • San Francisco • London

Chairman: Kevin Weldon
President: John Owen
Publisher: Sheena Coupe
Managing Editor: Ariana Klepac
Art Director: Sue Burk
Senior Designer: Mark Thacker
Designer: Regina Safro
Text Editors: Robert Coupe, Paulette Kay
Text Advisers: Mr. Phil Coleman, Dr. Bruce B. Collette,
Dr. Allan E. Greer, Dr. Jeff M. Leis, Dr. John R. Paxton,
Dr. Victor G. Springer
Photo Researcher: Elizabeth Connolly
Production Director: Mick Bagnato
Production Manager: Simone Perryman

Film production by Mandarin Offset
Printed in Mexico

SEA
CREATURES

PROFESSOR FRANK H. TALBOT
AND DR. JAMES G. MEAD

NATIONAL
GEOGRAPHIC
SOCIETY

INTRODUCTION

Many amazing creatures live in our oceans. There are warm-blooded, air-breathing mammals, such as whales, dolphins, seals, sea lions, and sea otters, as well as cold-blooded reptiles and fishes, and soft-bodied mollusks, like squid.

Some feed in the warm waters near the surface, while others swim in the cold, dark depths along the ocean floor. Some shelter in bays and harbors, and others travel huge distances at high speeds to find food or places to breed.

This book looks at just some of the sea creatures you might see from the beach, from a boat, washed up on the shore, or even in an aquarium. Always take care when you find sea creatures in rock pools or on the beach. Many have tentacles or sharp spines that can give a painful sting. A few sea-dwelling mammals don't seem to mind human company, whereas others swim away as

soon as people
come too near.

It's best to watch
and learn about
these wonderful
underwater animals from a
distance. Keeping our seas free
from pollution will help make sure
that we can do this for years to come.

HOW TO USE THIS BOOK

Each spread in this book helps you to
identify one kind of sea creature. It gives
you information about the creature's size,
color, appearance, and behavior. "Where To
Find" has a map of waters around North
America. It shows the sea creature's range.
The entry also describes its habitat.

Discover an unusual fact about
the creature in the
"Field Note," and see it
in its natural environment
in the photograph. If you find
a word you do not know, you can
look it up in the Glossary on page 76.

WHALE SHARK

Whale sharks are the world's largest fish. They have wide, flat heads and enormous, slitlike mouths. They glide silently through coastal waters, filtering plankton and shrimp through their gills.

WHERE TO FIND:

Whale sharks feed near the surface in the warm waters of the world's oceans.

WHAT TO LOOK FOR:

✳ SIZE
A whale shark is about 60 feet long and weighs up to 15 tons.

✳ COLOR
It is mostly brown, with paler spots and stripes on its back and sides.

✳ OTHER FEATURES
It has three long ridges along each side.

✳ BEHAVIOR
Like all fish, the whale shark has gills on each side of its head, which it breathes through. The gills look like slits.

The huge body of a whale shark provides shelter for small pilot fish.

BASKING SHARK

 A basking shark swims near the surface of the sea with its mouth wide open. Inside it, hundreds of long, fine bristles, called gill rakers, trap plankton and tiny shrimp, which the shark swallows.

WHERE TO FIND:
Basking sharks live in cool, shallow water in all the world's oceans. They feed close to the shore.

WHAT TO LOOK FOR:

✳ SIZE
Basking sharks grow about 30 feet long. They weigh up to 4 tons.

✳ COLOR
They have either blue, brown, or black backs, with paler bellies.

✳ OTHER FEATURES
They filter up to a thousand tons of water per hour through their gill rakers.

✳ BEHAVIOR
They are rarely seen in winter. Scientists think they hibernate on the seafloor.

The basking shark's gill rakers are the dark patches between its white gills.

WHITE SHARK

White sharks have huge jaws and sharp teeth. They usually hunt alone, cruising the coastlines for seals, sea lions, and fish to eat. They sometimes follow ocean liners, looking for food scraps.

WHERE TO FIND:
White sharks hunt mostly near the shore in all the world's oceans, except in the earth's coldest areas.

WHAT TO LOOK FOR:

✷ SIZE
White sharks grow to about 21 feet long and weigh more than 3 tons.

✷ COLOR
They have blue-gray backs and white bellies.

✷ OTHER FEATURES
Like other sharks, they can pick up weak electrical signals given off by fish.

✷ BEHAVIOR
They lift their heads out of the water to look for seals and sea lions on the shore.

Because they have pointed snouts, white sharks are also called white pointers.

FIELD NOTES

A white shark may mistake a surfer wearing flippers for a seal or a sea lion.

HAMMERHEAD SHARK

 Hammerheads are strong swimmers. They swing their heads from side to side as they search the seafloor for buried stingrays. Their sharp teeth can bite a fish in half.

WHERE TO FIND:
Hammerheads live in all oceans. They usually swim in warmer water, close to the coast.

WHAT TO LOOK FOR:

* SIZE
A hammerhead can be 14 feet long and weigh more than 1,000 pounds.

* COLOR
It has a grayish back and a white belly.

* OTHER FEATURES
Hammerheads have good vision and a strong sense of smell.

* BEHAVIOR
Hammerheads often get stingray spikes stuck in their mouths. These do not seem to harm them.

The hammerhead shark has an eye and a nostril on each end of its wide snout.

FIELD NOTES

Hammerheads pick up electrical signals given off by stingrays hiding under the sand.

SKATE

Skates appear to fly through the sea. They are related to rays. They have plate-shaped bodies, and mottled patterns on their backs that blend in perfectly with their surroundings on the seafloor.

WHERE TO FIND:
Skates live near the bottom in all oceans, but they are rare in some parts of the Pacific.

WHAT TO LOOK FOR:

✳ SIZE
Skates can be up to eight feet long and are about six feet from side to side.

✳ COLOR
They have brown backs and white bellies.

✳ OTHER FEATURES
A female skate lays eggs in a leathery egg case called a "mermaid's purse," where the eggs are kept until they hatch.

✳ BEHAVIOR
Skates swim by waving their side fins or "wings." They steer with their tails.

A skate has rough, spiny skin. Some have large, round spots on their backs.

SAWFISH

A sawfish has a broad, sawlike snout, with up to 30 hard, sharp teeth along each side. It swims through schools of mullet, sardines, and other fish, slashing its saw from side to side.

WHERE TO FIND:
Sawfish live in warm, shallow waters along the East Coast. They may also swim into rivers.

WHAT TO LOOK FOR:

✳ SIZE
A sawfish can be over 23 feet long.

✳ COLOR
Sawfish have brown backs and pale bellies.

✳ OTHER FEATURES
Sawfish are related to rays. Like rays, the sawfish has gill slits on the underside of its head.

✳ BEHAVIOR
A sawfish digs up crabs from the seafloor with its snout.

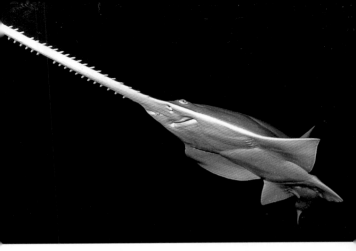

A sawfish gives birth to up to 23 babies. They hatch from eggs inside the mother's body.

ELECTRIC RAY

An electric ray has a flat body and a short tail. It has special organs that work like flashlight batteries in its large side fins. These can produce enough electricity to stun a five-pound fish.

WHERE TO FIND:
Various kinds of electric ray are found along the east and west coasts of North America.

WHAT TO LOOK FOR:

✳ SIZE
Electric rays are about six feet long.

✳ COLOR
They have yellowish backs and pale bellies. Some have speckles and spots.

✳ OTHER FEATURES
They have small, pointed teeth. They eat fish and shellfish from the seafloor.

✳ BEHAVIOR
Electric rays hide in sand. They wait for fish to swim overhead, then they stun the prey with an electric shock.

This bull's-eye electric ray has spots and circles on its back.

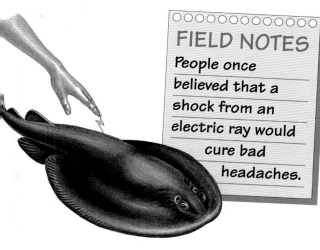

EAGLE RAY

Eagle rays feed on clams and small fish that shelter in the giant seaweed, called kelp, along coastlines. They are fast swimmers and have long, whiplike tails with one or two poisonous spines.

WHERE TO FIND:
Eagle rays swim in warm, shallow waters along the east and west coasts of North America.

WHAT TO LOOK FOR:

✳ SIZE
Eagle rays grow about nine feet across.

✳ COLOR
Some have gray-brown backs, with white, yellow, or blue spots. Their bellies are white.

✳ OTHER FEATURES
Eagle rays have small teeth for crushing clam shells.

✳ BEHAVIOR
Eagle rays leap out of the water and fall back to the surface with a splash.

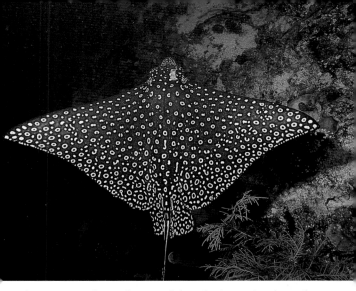

The spotted eagle ray blends into its coral reef surroundings.

FIELD NOTES

Hunters once used the poisonous tail spines of eagle rays to tip arrows or spears.

MANTA RAY

The manta is the giant of all the rays. It "flies" underwater with long sweeps of its huge fins. As it swims, its hornlike feeding fins guide plankton, shrimp, and small fish into its wide mouth.

WHERE TO FIND:
Manta rays swim near the surface of the warm and cooler waters of all the world's oceans.

WHAT TO LOOK FOR:

✳ SIZE
A manta ray's wingspan can measure 21 feet. It can weigh over 1 1/2 tons.

✳ COLOR
A manta ray has a dark gray back and a white belly.

✳ OTHER FEATURES
It has only one set of teeth—in its lower jaw.

✳ BEHAVIOR
Manta rays eat plankton, small shrimp, and fish.

Because they have long "horns" on their heads, manta rays are sometimes called devilfish.

TARPON

Tarpons have huge mouths, large scales, and forked tails. Fossils of their ancestors have been found in rocks that are 100 million years old. They feed on crayfish, crabs, and fish.

WHERE TO FIND:

Tarpons swim in the warm, tropical waters off the east coast of North America, and sometimes in bays.

WHAT TO LOOK FOR:

❋ SIZE
Tarpons are about 8 feet long, and can weigh up to 350 pounds.

❋ COLOR
Tarpons are a shimmering silver color.

❋ OTHER FEATURES
They have long filaments that trail like streamers from their back fins. Scientists think these might help them to swim.

❋ BEHAVIOR
Tarpons gulp air from the surface when there is not enough oxygen in the water.

Tarpons have large, silvery scales, and are sometimes called silver kings.

FIELD NOTES
Tarpons can leap right out of the water. They have even landed in fishermen's boats.

CONGER EEL

 Conger (KONG-ger) eels have long, snakelike bodies and powerful jaws, which they use to grip and eat their prey. They travel huge distances to breed in the deep waters of the open ocean.

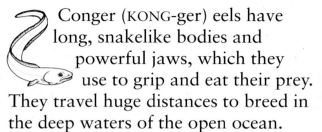

WHERE TO FIND:

There are a hundred types of conger eels. They are spread throughout all the world's oceans.

WHAT TO LOOK FOR:

✳ **SIZE**
Large conger eels can be up to 9 feet long and weigh 160 pounds.

✳ **COLOR**
They have dark gray to black backs and pale gray or white bellies.

✳ **OTHER FEATURES**
Conger eel larvae (LAR-vee) are large, flat, and see-through when they hatch.

✳ **BEHAVIOR**
Conger eels feed mostly at night, on cuttlefish, fish, and other conger eels.

Conger eels sometimes shelter in shipwrecks that lie on reefs.

BARRACUDA

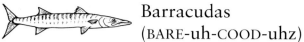

Barracudas (BARE-uh-COOD-uhz) are ocean predators with long, pointed jaws and huge, daggerlike teeth. They charge at schools of mullet and other fish with lightning speed.

FIELD NOTES
Barracudas have long teeth in the roofs of their mouths that they use to stab small fish.

WHERE TO FIND:
Barracudas live around coral reefs off both the east and west coasts of North America.

WHAT TO LOOK FOR:

✳ **SIZE**
The largest barracuda is about 6 feet long, and can weigh up to 100 pounds.

✳ **COLOR**
A barracuda has silver sides, a greenish-blue or gray back, and a white belly.

✳ **OTHER FEATURES**
It has sharp teeth for stabbing and small teeth for shredding.

✳ **BEHAVIOR**
Small cleaner wrasse fish clean bacteria and parasites off a barracuda's teeth.

The great barracuda waits for fish and other prey to drift past, usually over coral reefs.

BLUEFIN TUNA

Bluefin tuna are large and powerful fish that can swim long distances at very high speed. They travel across the world's oceans looking for schools of herring and other small fish.

WHERE TO FIND:
The bluefin tuna swims far out to sea in the North Atlantic and Pacific Oceans.

WHAT TO LOOK FOR:

✳ SIZE
A bluefin tuna grows 10 feet long and can weigh up to 1,500 pounds.

✳ COLOR
It is blue-black on the back and sides, and silvery white on the belly.

✳ OTHER FEATURES
One female can produce more than ten million eggs in one year.

✳ BEHAVIOR
At breeding time, bluefin tuna gather in large schools in special places.

Bluefin tuna have thick rounded bodies, powerful forked tails, and blue fins.

BLUE MARLIN

 The blue marlin is huge and one of the fastest of all fish. It can race through the water at almost 70 miles an hour, striking out at schools of fish with its sharp, spearlike bill.

WHERE TO FIND:
Blue marlins live along the coasts of North and Central America. They also migrate out to sea.

WHAT TO LOOK FOR:

＊SIZE
Blue marlins can be 15 feet long and weigh about 1 ton.

＊COLOR
They are brownish blue, with shiny silver sides.

＊OTHER FEATURES
Blue marlins have small, needlelike scales embedded in their skin.

＊BEHAVIOR
They sometimes pierce the hulls of wooden boats with their powerful bills.

Blue marlins often eat tuna. They spear
them with their huge bills.

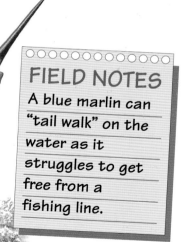

FIELD NOTES

A blue marlin can
"tail walk" on the
water as it
struggles to get
free from a
fishing line.

GREAT OCEAN SUNFISH

 An ocean sunfish has a round body and almost no tail, which makes it look like a large, floating ball. It uses its side fins like oars to move slowly, but steadily, through the water.

WHERE TO FIND:
Ocean sunfish live in waters along the coasts and far out to sea. You may see them from boats.

WHAT TO LOOK FOR:

✳ **SIZE**
An ocean sunfish can be ten feet long and weigh up to one ton.

✳ **COLOR**
It is brownish gray or black all over, with pale spots on its fins.

✳ **OTHER FEATURES**
It has leathery skin over thick layers of gristle.

✳ **BEHAVIOR**
A female ocean sunfish lays up to 28 million tiny eggs in the breeding season.

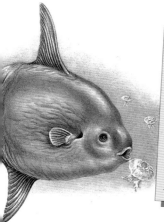

Instead of separate teeth, each jaw of an ocean sunfish is lined with a single, solid tooth plate.

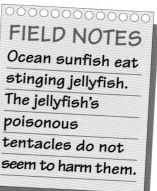

GIANT SQUID

 A giant squid is not a fish but a mollusk. This means it has a soft body and no backbone. It has ten long tentacles with suckers, and a parrotlike beak. It can live up to two miles under the sea.

FIELD NOTES

The Kraken, a mythical sea monster that sank ships, may be based on the giant squid.

WHERE TO FIND:
Giant squids live in all oceans, except the world's coldest waters. You may find one washed up on a beach.

WHAT TO LOOK FOR:

* **SIZE**
A giant squid can grow 50 feet long, and weigh up to a thousand pounds.

* **COLOR**
Its back and tentacles are purplish red.

* **OTHER FEATURES**
It has the largest eyes of any animal— larger than a car's headlights.

* **BEHAVIOR**
It sprays a cloud of black ink out of the funnel under its head when it is being chased by a predator.

The giant squid moves by sucking in water and then forcing it out again through a funnel underneath its head.

LEATHERBACK TURTLE

 Leatherback turtles are the largest living sea turtles. They have tough, leathery skin instead of bony shells. Their powerful front flippers help them to swim well.

WHERE TO FIND:
Leatherback turtles are reptiles that live in the cool and tropical waters of all the world's oceans.

WHAT TO LOOK FOR:

✳ SIZE
Leatherback turtles are about ten feet long and weigh nearly one ton.

✳ COLOR
They have brown or black shells, often with white spots.

✳ OTHER FEATURES
They have sharp beaks with which they grasp jellyfish, starfish, and shellfish.

✳ BEHAVIOR
They can dive to depths of a thousand feet when searching for food.

The female leatherback turtle always returns to the same beach where it was born to lay her eggs.

RIGHT WHALE

 Like all other whales, dolphins, and porpoises, right whales are mammals. Right whales were once hunted for their baleen and valuable oil. Whalers believed they were the correct, or "right," whales to catch.

WHERE TO FIND:
Right whales breed off the Florida coast, and live in the coastal water of all the world's oceans.

WHAT TO LOOK FOR:

✳ SIZE
Adult right whales can be 60 feet long.

✳ COLOR
They are black all over. Some have white patches on their bellies.

✳ OTHER FEATURES
They have comblike plates, called baleen, in their top jaws through which they filter small fish and shrimp from the water.

✳ BEHAVIOR
They gather in large groups, to feed in summer, and to breed in winter.

Right whales, like all whales, dolphins, and porpoises, breathe through holes in the tops of their heads, called blowholes.

41

GRAY WHALE

Gray whales are the only whales that swim along the bottom to feed. They plow through the mud on the ocean floor, filtering out mouthfuls of tiny sea creatures through their baleen.

WHERE TO FIND:
The gray whale is one of the few kinds of whales that come into shallow water, so you can see it from the shore.

WHAT TO LOOK FOR:

✳ **SIZE**
Female gray whales grow up to 46 feet long and weigh 34 tons. Males are slightly smaller.

✳ **COLOR**
They are mottled gray and white.

✳ **OTHER FEATURES**
Their skin looks blotchy because of barnacles and whale lice that grow on it.

✳ **BEHAVIOR**
Gray whales, like some other whales, come into sheltered bays to give birth.

Gray whales will let whale-watchers in boats come up close to them.

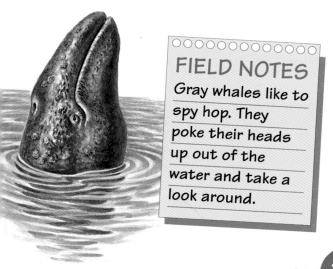

FIELD NOTES

Gray whales like to spy hop. They poke their heads up out of the water and take a look around.

BLUE WHALE

 Blue whales are the largest animals ever known to have lived. They roam alone or in groups of two or three. Each day, a blue whale filters as much as four tons of tiny shrimp through its baleen.

WHERE TO FIND:
Blue whales live in the cool parts of all the oceans of the world. They usually stay far away from the shore.

WHAT TO LOOK FOR:

✳ SIZE
An adult blue whale is about 85 feet long, and weighs about 100 tons.

✳ COLOR
Blue whales are blue-gray, with light gray spots all over.

✳ OTHER FEATURES
A blue whale's heart is about the size of a small car.

✳ BEHAVIOR
A newborn can drink a hundred gallons of its mother's milk in a day.

The blow, or spout, of a blue whale sprays as high as 30 feet into the air.

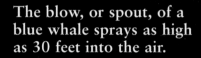

FIELD NOTES

A large blue whale can weigh as much as 20 African elephants or 2,300 adult humans.

HUMPBACK WHALE

 Male humpbacks communicate by singing eerie underwater songs. Like right whales, humpbacks leap out of the water and fall back with a huge splash. This is called breaching.

WHERE TO FIND:
Humpbacks live in all the world's oceans. They migrate to tropical waters in winter.

WHAT TO LOOK FOR:

❋ **SIZE**
Adults are about 45 feet long and weigh as much as 30 small cars.

❋ **COLOR**
Humpbacks are black with white markings on the underside.

❋ **OTHER FEATURES**
Like other baleen whales, humpbacks have two blowholes.

❋ **BEHAVIOR**
Like all baleen whales, they filter food through the baleen in their top jaws.

Humpbacks have enormous flippers which are about 15 feet long—almost one third of the total body length.

SPERM WHALE

 These gigantic toothed whales may eat up to one ton of food a day. Sperm whales were once hunted for the waxy oil, called spermaceti, found in a cavity inside their enormous heads.

WHERE TO FIND:
Sperm whales spend most of their time in the deepest parts of the world's oceans.

WHAT TO LOOK FOR:

✳ SIZE
Sperm whales grow as long as 60 feet, and weigh about 50 tons.

✳ COLOR
Most are dark gray with white patches on the belly.

✳ OTHER FEATURES
They catch slippery squid with their sharp teeth.

✳ BEHAVIOR
Females communicate more often than males do. They make clicking sounds.

The sperm whale has the largest head of any animal. The head may be 20 feet long.

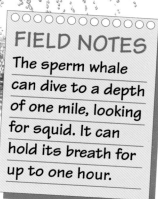

FIELD NOTES

The sperm whale can dive to a depth of one mile, looking for squid. It can hold its breath for up to one hour.

BELUGA

Belugas (buh-LOO-guhz) sometimes swim upside down. Long ago, sailors called them "sea canaries" because they could hear the belugas' whistling calls echoing through the hull of a boat.

WHERE TO FIND:
Belugas swim mainly in shallow seas and rivers in the Arctic region. Some live farther south.

WHAT TO LOOK FOR:

✳ **SIZE**
Belugas are about 15 feet long, and weigh as much as 2 horses.

✳ **COLOR**
They are born dark gray. By the age of five or six, they are completely white.

✳ **OTHER FEATURES**
Unlike most whales, belugas can move their heads from side to side.

✳ **BEHAVIOR**
They pucker their lips to suck in food. They eat fish, squid, crabs, and shrimp.

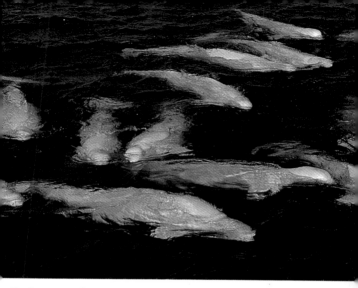

Belugas often travel in large groups of around 200 to 300. They are also known as white whales.

FIELD NOTES

Belugas have very flexible muscles, especially in their faces. Sometimes they look as if they are "making faces."

NARWHAL

 The male narwhal (NAR-WALL) has a long, spiral tusk growing through its upper lip. This tusk is actually an overgrown tooth. Females have teeth, but they hardly ever grow beyond the jaw.

WHERE TO FIND:
Narwhals live in icy Arctic waters. They usually feed in the deep ocean, far away from land.

WHAT TO LOOK FOR:

☀ **SIZE**
Males can grow to be 15 feet long. Their tusks can grow to 9 feet— almost the length of a basketball pole.

☀ **COLOR**
The young are light gray all over. Adults are mottled gray and white.

☀ **OTHER FEATURES**
Their favorite foods are fish and squid.

☀ **BEHAVIOR**
Narwhals often go hunting for food in groups of six to ten.

Some scientists believe that males use their tusks in fights with other males, to guard territory or to win a mate.

Baby

Female

COMMON DOLPHIN

 Dolphins (DOL-finz), like porpoises, are a kind of whale. Common dolphins hunt in large groups and sometimes reach speeds of 30 miles an hour, especially when they are chasing flying fish for food.

WHERE TO FIND:
Common dolphins live in warm to cool waters near the coasts, as well as in the open sea.

WHAT TO LOOK FOR:

✳ SIZE
An adult common dolphin is about 8 feet long and weighs over 150 pounds.

✳ COLOR
It has a black back and a yellowish-brown stripe on each side.

✳ OTHER FEATURES
It has about 200 small, pointed teeth that it uses to grip its prey.

✳ BEHAVIOR
Common dolphins feed on anchovies, herring, sardines, and squid.

A common dolphin has a sickle-shaped fin on its back and two long, slender flippers that help it to swim fast.

FIELD NOTES

Common dolphins leap into the air as they ride the bow waves of ships and, sometimes, of large whales.

PILOT WHALE

 Sometimes several hundred pilot whales strand themselves on a beach and die. No one is sure why this happens. Perhaps the leader swims too close to shore and the others follow.

WHERE TO FIND:
Pilot whales usually swim in the open ocean. They also come closer to the coast in summer.

WHAT TO LOOK FOR:

✳ **SIZE**
Pilot whales are about 20 feet long and weigh up to 6,000 pounds.

✳ **COLOR**
They are mainly black, with white patches on the throat and belly.

✳ **OTHER FEATURES**
Like all toothed whales, pilot whales have single blowholes.

✳ **BEHAVIOR**
They often travel in huge pods of up to 2,000. Their favorite food is squid.

Because of their rounded foreheads, pilot whales are also known as potheads.

FIELD NOTES

Male pilot whales sometimes bump each other with their heads to fight for territory or to win a mate.

ATLANTIC WHITE-SIDED DOLPHIN

 Atlantic white-sided dolphins swim fast and often jump into the air as they ride the waves that big ships make. This is why they are also called "jumpers."

WHERE TO FIND:
These dolphins live in the cooler waters of the Atlantic Ocean, far out to sea.

WHAT TO LOOK FOR:

❋ **SIZE**
White-sided dolphins have small flippers, and grow about eight feet long.

❋ **COLOR**
They are gray with a white underside, white streaks on the back and sides, and a patch of yellow on each side of the tail.

❋ **OTHER FEATURES**
White-sided dolphins have a short snout and 30 to 40 teeth.

❋ **BEHAVIOR**
They usually travel in pods of 10 to 50.

Atlantic white-sided dolphins communicate with each other by making clicking and whistling sounds.

000000000000000

FIELD NOTES

Sometimes up to 1,000 white-sided dolphins will band together to hunt for herring and squid.

59

BOTTLENOSE DOLPHIN

 Bottlenose dolphins are the dolphins you most often see from the shore. They have streamlined bodies and short flippers, and can swim very fast.

WHERE TO FIND:

Bottlenose dolphins live in the warmer waters of all oceans. They often come into bays and harbors.

WHAT TO LOOK FOR:

✳ SIZE
A bottlenose dolphin can grow to 13 feet long.

✳ COLOR
It has a dark gray back, lighter gray sides, and a pinkish white belly.

✳ OTHER FEATURES
It has a short beak that looks a little like the neck of a bottle.

✳ BEHAVIOR
Bottlenose dolphins send messages to each other by whistling and squealing.

A bottlenose dolphin has a single blowhole.

HARBOR PORPOISE

 Although there are large numbers of harbor porpoises (POR-puh-suhz), they are rarely seen. They come to the water's surface to breathe, then dive underwater again with hardly a splash.

WHERE TO FIND:
Harbor porpoises live in cool, coastal waters throughout the Northern Hemisphere.

WHAT TO LOOK FOR:

✳ SIZE
Harbor porpoises grow about 6 feet long and weigh about 200 pounds.

✳ COLOR
They are dark gray to brown black, with light-gray bellies.

✳ OTHER FEATURES
Harbor porpoises have small mouths, and spade-shaped teeth.

✳ BEHAVIOR
They feed on fish, such as mackerel and herring, and on squid and shrimp.

The harbor porpoise, which is also called the common porpoise, has a flat forehead and rounded flippers.

CALIFORNIA SEA LION

 California sea lions twist and tumble among kelp forests near the Pacific coast. They use their big, round eyes and sensitive whiskers to hunt for squid and octopus.

WHERE TO FIND:
California sea lions live in water close to the Pacific coast. They often bask on rocks.

WHAT TO LOOK FOR:

✳ SIZE
Males can be 7 feet long and weigh 800 pounds. Females are about as long, but weigh only 250 pounds.

✳ COLOR
They are tan to dark brown.

✳ OTHER FEATURES
They have ear flaps covering their ear openings to keep the water out.

✳ BEHAVIOR
Sea lions gather in noisy, crowded colonies on rocky coastlines.

California sea lions swim with their front flippers. Their relatives, seals, use their back flippers.

WALRUS

 Walruses use their tusks and whiskers to search the seafloor for shellfish. They have layers of fat, called blubber, under their skin to help keep them warm in freezing waters.

WHERE TO FIND:
Walruses live in shallow waters in and around the Arctic. They bask in large herds on pack ice there.

WHAT TO LOOK FOR:

✳ **SIZE**
Male walruses are about 10 feet long and weigh 3 tons. Females are smaller, at about 8 feet and 2,000 pounds.

✳ **COLOR**
Walruses are tan to light brown.

✳ **OTHER FEATURES**
Males make strange, bell-like sounds under the water to attract mates.

✳ **BEHAVIOR**
Walruses suck clams out of the shells without even breaking them open.

Male walruses often have scars and scratches from fights with other males.

FIELD NOTES

Walruses gather in large groups to breed. Often, thousands huddle together in huge piles.

HARP SEAL

Harp seals are speedy swimmers. In early spring, tens of thousands of them wriggle on their bellies over the slippery pack ice to breed. They eat fish, squid, octopus, and shrimp.

WHERE TO FIND:

Harp seals swim in the North Atlantic Ocean. During spring, they live on floating pack ice.

WHAT TO LOOK FOR:

✳ SIZE
Harp seals can grow 7 feet long and weigh about 300 pounds.

✳ COLOR
An adult has a black head and a white body. The seal gets its name from the harp-shaped patch on its back.

✳ OTHER FEATURES
Like all seals, they live in large groups.

✳ BEHAVIOR
They dive to the seafloor to find food. Pups can swim two weeks after birth.

Harp seals send messages to each other by barking, grunting, and squeaking.

69

HARBOR SEAL

 Harbor seals spend most of their time looking for fish and squid. They give birth on land and quickly return to the sea. Unlike most seals, they look after their pups alone or in small groups.

WHERE TO FIND:
Harbor seals swim in shallow coastal waters. They often float on logs or bask on beaches.

WHAT TO LOOK FOR:

✳ **SIZE**
Harbor seals are about 6 feet long. Males weigh around 300 pounds, and females weigh about half that.

✳ **COLOR**
They have dark gray to brown backs, and white bellies.

✳ **OTHER FEATURES**
Their fur has spots, rings, and blotches.

✳ **BEHAVIOR**
Harbor seals are quite timid. They bark and growl if intruders get too near.

Like all seals, a harbor seal has ear openings that are not covered by ear flaps.

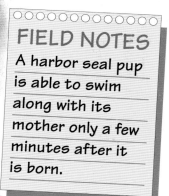

FIELD NOTES

A harbor seal pup is able to swim along with its mother only a few minutes after it is born.

SEA OTTER

 Sea otters are mammals that spend almost all their lives in the sea. They swim near the water's surface, darting over and under kelp beds, searching for clams and other seafood.

WHERE TO FIND:
Sea otters live in beds of kelp, close to rocky coasts. They are the same color as kelp, so they are hard to see.

WHAT TO LOOK FOR:

✳ SIZE
Sea otters are as big as medium-size dogs. They weigh up to 80 pounds.

✳ COLOR
They have brown fur. As they get older, their head fur becomes lighter.

✳ OTHER FEATURES
Sea otters have long tails, webbed front feet, and flippers instead of back feet.

✳ BEHAVIOR
They sleep and give birth while floating on the surface of the sea.

Female sea otters often make cooing sounds to their pups. When disturbed, they hiss or growl.

WEST INDIAN MANATEE

 Manatees (MAN-uh-TEEZ) are large, bulky mammals. They swim slowly near the surface of the water, busily munching on sea grass and other water plants.

WHERE TO FIND:
Manatees live in shallow, coastal waters in tropical oceans and rivers. In winter they swim in warm springs.

WHAT TO LOOK FOR:

✳ SIZE
Manatees grow to a length of 15 feet and weigh as much as a cow.

✳ COLOR
They are medium gray. Some have white blotches on their bellies.

✳ OTHER FEATURES
They have tough skin, small front flippers, and a broad, flat tail.

✳ BEHAVIOR
In winter they sometimes swim in the warm water near power stations.

A manatee calf drinks milk from its mother's teats. Mothers chirp, whistle, and squeal to their calves.

○○○○○○○○○○○○○○
FIELD NOTES
The manatee and
the elephant are
related. They are
both herbivores
and both have
tough skin.

GLOSSARY

Bacteria Tiny living creatures that can only be seen through a microscope. Some bacteria spread disease.

Barnacle A small, shrimplike creature with a shell that often clings to the bottoms of boats or lives on the skin of whales.

Bask When an animal lies in the sun to warm its body and get the energy it needs to move around.

Bill The long beak of a sea creature or bird.

Breed To produce young.

Communicate To send messages.

Gill rakers The long, fine bristles on the gills of some fish that are used to strain tiny animals and plants from the water for food.

Herbivore An animal that eats only plants.

Hibernate When an animal sleeps through the winter so it does not need to eat.

Hull The framework of a boat.

Mammal A warm-blooded animal. The young feed on milk from the mother's body. Most mammals have hair or fur except for whales, dolphins, and porpoises.

Mate An adult creature's male or female partner with which it produces young.

Organ A part of the body, such as the heart or brain, that helps the body to function.

Oxygen A gas that all animals need to breathe to live.

Parasite An animal or plant that lives in or on another animal and gets its food from that body.

Plankton The tiny animals and plants that drift about in huge groups in the surface waters of the ocean.

Pod The word for a group of whales.

Predator Any creature that hunts other creatures for food.

Prey Any creature hunted by other creatures for food.

School The word for a group of fish.

Tentacles The long, thin feelers that squid and some other sea creatures use for grasping and feeding.

INDEX OF
SEA CREATURES

ABOUT THE CONSULTANTS

Dr. James G. Mead started his academic life as a vertebrate paleontologist, interested in fossil reptiles, but was diverted into the study of whales and dolphins. He is currently the Curator of Marine Mammals, National Museum of Natural History, Smithsonian Institution.

Professor Frank Talbot is a marine scientist and writer and has held many distinguished, academic positions including Director of the South African Museum in Cape Town, Director of the Australian Museum in Sydney, Director of the California Academy of Sciences in San Francisco, and Director of the Smithsonian Institution's National Museum of Natural History. He currently holds visiting chairs at the University of Sydney and Macquarie University.

PHOTOGRAPHIC CREDITS

front cover Francisco J. Erize/Bruce Coleman Ltd. **back cover** Carl Roessler/ Bruce Coleman Ltd. **half title page** Jeff Foott Productions/Bruce Coleman Ltd. 2–3 Frank Lane/Bruce Coleman Ltd. 4–5 Jeff Foott Productions/Bruce Coleman Ltd. 5 Richard Herrmann/Oxford Scientific Films 7 Gary Bell/ Australian Picture Library 9 Howard Hall/Oxford Scientific Films 11 Carl Roessler/Bruce Coleman Ltd. 13 Flip Nicklin/Minden Pictures 15 Jeffrey L. Rotman/Peter Arnold, Inc. 17 Norbert Wu/Planet Earth Pictures 19 James L. Watt/Planet Earth Pictures 21 Capt. Clay H. Wiseman/Animals Animals 23 Howard Hall/Oxford Scientific Films 25 Peter Scoones/Planet Earth Pictures 27 Kurt Amsler/Planet Earth Pictures 28–29 Marty Snyderman/ Planet Earth Pictures 31 Norbert Wu 33 James D. Watt/Planet Earth Pictures 35 Richard Herrmann/Oxford Scientific Films 37 Alex Kerstitch/Planet Earth Pictures 39 Jany Sauvanet/Auscape International 41 Flip Nicklin/Minden Pictures 43 Pieter Folkens/Planet Earth Pictures 45 Flip Nicklin/Minden Pictures 47 James D. Watt/Planet Earth Pictures 49 Howard Hall/Oxford Scientific Films 51 Flip Nicklin/Minden Pictures 53 Flip Nicklin/Minden Pictures 55 Flip Nicklin/Minden Pictures 57 Flip Nicklin/Minden Pictures 59 Hugh Clark/FLPA 61 Flip Nicklin/Minden Pictures 63 Eric Dorfman 65 David Fleetham/Oxford Scientific Films 67 Hans Reinhard/Bruce Coleman Ltd. 69 Hans Reinhard/Bruce Coleman Ltd. 71 David S. Boyer/ NGS Image Collection 73 Daniel J. Cox/Oxford Scientific Films 75 Doug Perrine/Planet Earth Pictures 76 Flip Nicklin/Minden Pictures 77 Doug Perrine/Planet Earth Pictures 78 John Murray/Bruce Coleman Ltd. 79 (**top**) Charles & Sandra Hood/Bruce Coleman Ltd. 79 (**bottom**) Leonard Lee Rue/Bruce Coleman Ltd.